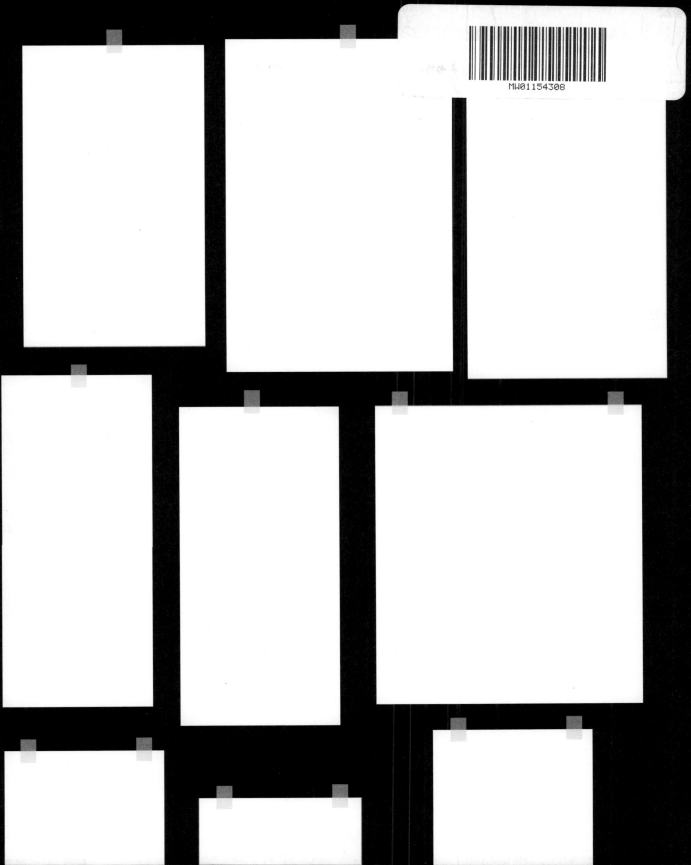

Little People, **BIG DREAMS**™

YVES SAINT LAURENT

Written by
Maria Isabel Sánchez Vegara

Illustrated by
Klas Fahlén

Frances Lincoln
Children's Books

In the city of Oran, in Algeria, there lived a quiet boy named Yves who had a great sense of style. He was fascinated by his mother's clothes and loved to draw pretty dresses for his little sister's dolls.

Yves' family always encouraged him to be himself,
but at school he was bullied for being different.

Many days, he pretended to be sick so he could stay in his room and avoid the mean comments from other children.

During his teenage years, Yves began to sew tiny outfits.
He used scraps of fabric from his mom's clothes
and dressed up models cut out of fashion magazines.

He dreamed of becoming a couturier,
a luxury clothing designer.

His designs were so beautiful and detailed that, at seventeen, he placed third in a young designers contest. The following year, Yves moved to Paris, the capital of fashion, to study at the top couturier school.

One day, he was introduced to the most famous couturier of the time: Christian Dior.

Monsieur Dior was so impressed by Yves' talent that he asked him to be his assistant. Yves learned a lot from him and, little by little, gained Dior's trust.

Sadly, just two years later, Dior died.
Following the great designer's wishes, Yves took his
place and became the youngest couturier of the time.

When he presented his first collection,
everyone in the fashion world was watching.

Yves' first show was a success, and a guy named Pierre was one of the lucky attendees. When they met a couple of days later, Yves fell in love with this charming and clever young man. Their love story would last almost a lifetime.

Three years later, Yves was forced to join the French army, where some of the soldiers treated him badly. Yves was so upset he became unwell and had to stay in the hospital. There, he found out that he had been fired from Dior.

When he returned home, Pierre took care of him. Once Yves felt better, they were ready for a new adventure! They decided to set up their own fashion house, and many Dior employees, from models to seamstresses, joined them.

Yves' first design was a peacoat based on sailors' jackets. He thought women's clothes should be comfy and chic, so he took inspiration from the garments men wore. He even made pants for women, which was pretty unusual at the time.

Yves kept making expensive, handcrafted outfits in his studio.
But he wanted more people to be able to wear his clothes!

So, he created a more affordable collection,
which he sold in his new stores.

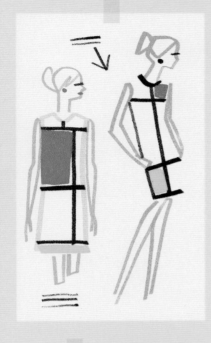

Few designers changed women's clothing like he did.
Yves designed tuxedo suits and colorful dresses inspired by
art and faraway places. He also introduced shoulder pads,
and safari jackets with lots of pockets, and he did it all in style!

After a lifetime of making beautiful clothes,
little Yves—the great prince of fashion—knew that the
secret to true style was feeling good in your own special way.

YVES SAINT LAURENT

(Born 1936 – Died 2008)

1958   1965

Yves Saint Laurent was born to a wealthy French family in Algeria, a French colony at the time. He was a shy, creative child who loved literature, theater, and fashion. At eighteen, he moved to Paris to study haute couture—luxury, handcrafted, made-to-order clothing. Within a year, the great couturier Christian Dior had spotted his remarkable talent and decided to hire him. When Dior died unexpectedly two years later, twenty-one-year-old Yves was announced as his successor—the world's youngest couturier! His first collection was an instant hit, but his next few flopped, and in 1960 he was called up for military service in Algeria, which was fighting to free itself from French rule. There, Yves suffered a mental-health crisis and soon after discovered he had lost his job at Dior. Encouraged by his partner,

1982

2001

Pierre Bergé, he started his own fashion company instead. Yves' visionary designs went on to revolutionize women's fashion. By taking inspiration from men's clothing, he popularized women wearing pants, tuxedos, jumpsuits, and other chic and comfortable garments. His dream, he said, was to design clothes that made women feel self-confident and happy. Yves was the first couturier to use Black models on the catwalk and one of the first to make high fashion more affordable, with a ready-to-wear collection launched in 1966. He was just forty-seven when the Metropolitan Museum of Art showcased his work in New York City—a great honor. And when he retired, thousands gathered to applaud his final show. Today, Yves is remembered as one of the greatest icons in fashion history.

Want to find out more?

Take a look at these great books:

Why Do We Wear Clothes? by Helen Hancocks (V&A)

The Culture of Clothes: A Celebration of World Dress
by Giovanna Alessio and Chaaya Prabhat

Published by Peter Marley · Edited by Molly Mead
Designed by Sasha Moxon and Izzy Bowman
Production by Robin Boothroyd
Manufactured in Guangdong, China CC012025
1 3 5 7 9 8 6 4 2

Photographic acknowledgments (pages 28-29, from left to right): 1. Yves Saint Laurent, Designer, Dior Fashion House, pictured at
the reception, Westbury Hotel, London, 11th November 1958. He will be showcasing his collection at Blenheim Palace, seat of the
Duke of Marlborough, in aid of the British Red Cross © Bob Hope / Mirrorpix via Getty Images. 2. Ready To Wear. 7th April 1965:
Yves Saint Laurent, ex-wonder boy of Dior, working with a fashion model at his own fashion house in Paris © Reg Lancaster / Stringer
/ Express / Hulton Archive via Getty Images. 3. French fashion designer Yves Saint Laurent (1936 – 2008) in his Paris studio, January
1982 © John Downing / Contributor / Hulton Archive via Getty Images. 4. Yves Saint Laurent walks on the catwalk at the YSL High
Fashion Show Autumn/Winter 2001-02 during fashion week 2001 in Paris, France © Michel Dufour / Contributor / WireImage /
French Select via Getty Images.

Collect the Little People, BIG DREAMS™ series:

FRIDA KAHLO	COCO CHANEL	MAYA ANGELOU	AMELIA EARHART	AGATHA CHRISTIE	MARIE CURIE	ROSA PARKS	AUDREY HEPBURN	EMMELINE PANKHURST
ELLA FITZGERALD	ADA LOVELACE	JANE AUSTEN	GEORGIA O'KEEFFE	HARRIET TUBMAN	ANNE FRANK	MOTHER TERESA	JOSEPHINE BAKER	L. M. MONTGOMERY
JANE GOODALL	SIMONE DE BEAUVOIR	MUHAMMAD ALI	STEPHEN HAWKING	MARIA MONTESSORI	VIVIENNE WESTWOOD	MAHATMA GANDHI	DAVID BOWIE	WILMA RUDOLPH
DOLLY PARTON	BRUCE LEE	RUDOLF NUREYEV	ZAHA HADID	MARY SHELLEY	MARTIN LUTHER KING JR.	DAVID ATTENBOROUGH	ASTRID LINDGREN	EVONNE GOOLAGONG
BOB DYLAN	ALAN TURING	BILLIE JEAN KING	GRETA THUNBERG	JESSE OWENS	JEAN-MICHEL BASQUIAT	ARETHA FRANKLIN	CORAZON AQUINO	PELÉ
ERNEST SHACKLETON	STEVE JOBS	AYRTON SENNA	LOUISE BOURGEOIS	ELTON JOHN	JOHN LENNON	PRINCE	CHARLES DARWIN	CAPTAIN TOM MOORE
HANS CHRISTIAN ANDERSEN	STEVIE WONDER	MEGAN RAPINOE	MARY ANNING	MALALA YOUSAFZAI	ANDY WARHOL	RUPAUL	MICHELLE OBAMA	MINDY KALING

IRIS APFEL	ROSALIND FRANKLIN	RUTH BADER GINSBURG	MARILYN MONROE	KAMALA HARRIS	ALBERT EINSTEIN	CHARLES DICKENS	YOKO ONO	MICHAEL JORDAN

NELSON MANDELA	PABLO PICASSO	AMANDA GORMAN	GLORIA STEINEM	FLORENCE NIGHTINGALE	HARRY HOUDINI	J.R.R. TOLKIEN	ELVIS PRESLEY	NEIL ARMSTRONG
ALEXANDER VON HUMBOLDT	NIKOLA TESLA	WILMA MANKILLER	MARCUS RASHFORD	LAVERNE COX	MAE JEMISON	DWAYNE JOHNSON	HELEN KELLER	ANNA PAVLOVA
QUEEN ELIZABETH	TERRY FOX	HEDY LAMARR	SHAKIRA	FREDDIE MERCURY	LEWIS HAMILTON	LOUIS PASTEUR	PRINCESS DIANA	DAVID HOCKNEY
VANESSA NAKATE	OLIVE MORRIS	KING CHARLES	MOZART	STEVE IRWIN	JÜRGEN KLOPP	LEO MESSI	SALLY RIDE	TENZING NORGAY
KYLIE MINOGUE	BEYONCÉ	TAYLOR SWIFT	RAFA NADAL	USAIN BOLT	SIMONE BILES	STAN LEE	LEONARD COHEN	VINCENT VAN GOGH
MARY KOM	SALVADOR DALÍ	ANTOINE DE SAINT-EXUPÉRY	DAVID BECKHAM	KATHERINE JOHNSON	PATRICK MAHOMES			
YAYOI KUSAMA	ROALD DAHL	HARRY STYLES	WILLIAM KAMKWAMBA	MARY EARPS	YVES SAINT LAURENT			

Scan the QR code for free activity sheets, teachers' notes and more information about the series at www.littlepeoplebigdreams.com